Pet Corner

SLITHERING SNAKES

By Rose Carraway

Gareth Stevens Publishing

Please visit our website, www.garethstevens.com. For a free color catalog of all our high-quality books, call toll free 1-800-542-2595 or fax 1-877-542-2596.

Library of Congress Cataloging-in-Publication Data

Carraway, Rose.
Slithering snakes / Rose Carraway.
p. cm. — (Pet corner)
Includes index.
ISBN 978-1-4339-6303-2 (pbk.)
ISBN 978-1-4339-6304-9 (6-pack)
ISBN 978-1-4339-6301-8 (library binding)
1. Snakes as pets—Juvenile literature. I. Title.
SF459.S5C36 2012
639.3'96—dc23

2011020898

First Edition

Published in 2012 by
Gareth Stevens Publishing
111 East 14th Street, Suite 349
New York, NY 10003

Editor: Katie Kawa
Designer: Andrea Davison-Bartolotta

Photo credits: Cover, pp. 1, 7, 9, 11, 13, 15, 19, 21, 24 (bowl, tongue) Shutterstock.com; p. 5 Michael Blann/Stone/Getty Images; p. 17 davespilbrow/Flickr/Getty Images; p. 23 Jupiterimages/Brand X Pictures/Thinkstock; p. 24 (cage) iStockphoto.com.

Printed in the United States of America

CPSIA compliance information: Batch #CW12GS: For further information contact Gareth Stevens, New York, New York at 1-800-542-2595.

Contents

Pet snakes come in many sizes. They can be many colors, too.

Snakes have no legs!

A pet snake lives
in a glass cage.

The cage needs
to be warm.

A snake likes
to feel safe.
It hides in its cage.

A pet snake needs
a water bowl.

It drinks the water.
It lies in the water, too.

Snakes eat other animals. They eat mice and rats.

A snake uses
its tongue to smell.
It works like a nose.

People can hold
pet snakes.
They have to be
very careful!

Words to Know

bowl

cage

tongue

Index